20

Most Asked Questions
about the
Amish and Mennonites

Merle and Phyllis Good

People's Place Book No. 1

Good Books

Intercourse, PA 17534
800/762-7171
www.goodbks.com

Acknowledgements

Statistics in Chapter 19 courtesy of Mennonite World Conference, Kitchener, Ontario; *The Mennonite Yearbook 1995* (Mennonite Publishing House); and Stephen Scott, researcher for The People's Place.

Photograph Credits

Front and back covers, Burton Buller; Daniel Price, 5; Burton Buller, 6 (right), 35, 85; Kenneth Pellman, 6 (left), 15 (bottom right), 57 (left), 76; Beth Oberholtzer, 7, 27 (both), 63, 67 (bottom); J.D. Stahl, 8 (both), 23; Jan Gleysteen, 11; Ed Huddle, 12; Merle Good, 15 (bottom left), 49, 75 (all), 81; *Hutchinson News,* 15 (top); Perry Cragg, 19 (top), 55; Fred Wilson, 19 (bottom), 40 (right), 65; Glenn Linscheid, 21; Peter Zimberg, 25, 72; Loris Habeggar collection, 29; Shawn Perry NISBCO, 31; Eastern Mennonite Board of Missions, 33; Dawn Ranck, 36; Richard Reinhold, 39, 51, 57 (right), 68, 71 (both); *Geauga Times Leader,* 40; Wide World Photos, 43; Kevin Shank, 45; Greg Bowman, 47; David Fretz, 53; David Hunsberger, 59; Mennonite Central Committee, 60 (right); Ray Yovanovich, 86; Jonathan Charles, 96

Design by Dawn J. Ranck

20 MOST ASKED QUESTIONS ABOUT THE AMISH AND MENNONITES
Copyright © 1979, 1995 by Good Books, Intercourse, PA 17534
Revised edition 1995
International Standard Book Number: 1-56148-185-8
Library of Congress Catalog Card Number: 95-37851

Library of Congress Cataloging-in-Publication Data

Good, Merle, 1946-
    20 most asked questions about the Amish and Mennonites / Merle and Phyllis Good. -- Rev. ed.
        p. cm. -- (People's Place book : no. 1)
    Includes bibliographical references and index.
    ISBN 1-56148-185-8
    1. Amish--Miscellanea. 2. Mennonites--Miscellanea. I. Good, Phyllis Pellman, 1948- . II. Title. III. Series: People's Place booklet ; no. 1.
    E184.M45G66   1995
    305.6'87--dc20   95-37851
                                                            CIP

Table of Contents

1.

What is the difference between the Amish and the Mennonites?

Anyone who tries to answer this question in one simple sentence is either naive or purposefully unkind.

Which of us would want our lives summed up in one sweeping statement? Yet many of us demand this of other people's lives.

The danger of generalizations

As authors, we must declare ourselves on the very first pages of this book. It is impossible to interpret the lives of a people—any people—in one or two quick sentences. It seems a violent act.

When a people become the object of curiosity and tourism as the Amish and the Mennonites have in various parts of North America, a lot of shallow, fast-buck, one-line interpretations appear.

There are dozens of varieties among the Amish and Mennonite groups around the world. Words like "always" and "never" seldom apply in describing the whole Mennonite-Amish family. On most of the topics we will cover in this book, there are many shades of belief and practice among our various groups.

There are dozens of Amish and Mennonite groups around the world, each with specific practices and beliefs. It is impossible to summarize these peoples' lives in one short sentence.

One issue which many of the groups approach differently is transportation. Old Order Amish buggies (center) in Lancaster County have grey tops. But Amish buggies vary in other communities across North America, both in shape and color. Some groups who drive cars illus-

Our purpose is to qualify generalizations while being as specific as possible. This can be frustrating. We will use the words "most" and "some" and "seldom" a great deal. Many readers will wish we would make more sweeping observations. But one-line generalizations create human zoos. People become spectacles.

The various Amish and Mennonite groups of Lancaster County, Pennsylvania are the central focus of our study. We will attempt throughout the book, however, to include information about the worldwide peoplehood.

In general

We will risk several generalizations at this point:

1. Most Mennonite and Amish groups have common his-

trate separation from worldliness by painting the chrome on their cars black (left photo). The photo on the right pictures a row of Old Order Mennonite buggies which have black tops.

torical roots. Their beginnings (1525) date from a group of persecuted radical Christians nicknamed "Anabaptists" at the time of the Protestant Reformation in Europe. They sought a return to the simplicity of faith and practice as seen in the early Christian church in the Bible. The Amish division took place a century and a half later in 1693. This history will be discussed in detail in the next chapter.

2. All Amish and Mennonite groups are Christian fellowships. Most of them stress that belief must result in practice. "By their fruits you shall know them" (Matthew 7:20). Therefore, emphases on lifestyle and peace have distinguished most of the groups throughout the centuries. More on this in Chapter 3.

3. The differences among the various Amish and Mennonite groups through the years have almost always been ones of practice rather than basic Christian doctrine. This is

Some groups such as the Old Order Amish and urban house fellowships worship in homes. Those who worship in churches vary from the simple three-quarter-round meetinghouse of the Old Order Mennonites to the more Protestant look of modern Mennonite sanctuaries.

not to minimize the differences, because they are real. But even today a survey of the whole family would show few differences on the Christian teaching of creation and redemption and a great many on how one should dress and how a congregation should make decisions.

More specifically

Amish groups tend to be more cautious on technology and involvement with the larger world than most Mennonites. Most Old Order Amish, for instance, drive horse-drawn carriages, dress "plain," refrain from the use of electricity, emphasize occupations close to the farm and the home, and forbid higher education. Many Mennonites, on the other hand, are considerably more acculturated. They embrace education and technology as opportunities, accept reluctantly the stress which modern life places on marriage and the family, and encourage an enlargement of the fellowship through worldwide missionary activities.

But this is very general. Thousands of Mennonites drive horses and buggies, avoid higher education, and are cautious on missions. And some Amish groups drive cars and encourage high school and mission work.

We find it more helpful for purposes of discussion to collect the many groups into two main categories: 1) those who take their cues for decision-making primarily from their faith fellowship, whom we shall refer to as "Old Order" (this may include many small urban groups who are "Old Order" in their dynamic); and 2) those who are more influenced in their primary decision-making by what the larger society thinks than by what their faith fellowship believes, whom we shall refer to as "modern."

These categories of "Old Order" and "modern" are much more helpful than "Mennonite" and "Amish" in describing the total family. In many cases, the Old Order Amish, the Old Order Mennonites, the Old Colony Mennonites, the Hutterites, and an inner-city Mennonite house church may share more in common than they do with more rapidly acculturating Mennonite and Amish groups.

In summary

One last comment. There are more similarities among the Mennonite-Amish fellowship worldwide than there are dissimilarities.

Obviously there are many differences, especially among the groups at the far edges of the spectrum. But there remain many unifying themes among the various Mennonite and Amish groups worldwide, even though the groups are organizationally independent.

The remainder of this book will explore both the differences and the likenesses of our peoples.

2.

When and how did these people get started?

All Amish and Mennonite groups trace their spiritual heritage back to the time of Christ and the early Christian church. The specific movement from which these groups descend, however, began on January 21, 1525 in Zurich, Switzerland.

The Anabaptists

When the Protestant Reformation broke open the religious world of sixteenth-century Europe, Martin Luther led the challenge against the Roman Church. At the same time, a Reformer named Ulrich Zwingli emerged in Zurich. Both men advocated a new Christian order. They preached the Bible in the language of the peasants and proclaimed that the grace of God and forgiveness of sins were available freely to all by faith alone. It was a time of great turmoil.

In the midst of this religious and social upheaval, a group who called themselves Brethren formed a fellowship. They were nicknamed Anabaptists (which means "rebaptizers"). They became severely persecuted by both the church of Rome and the Reformers. Why? Because they represented a third option: a belief that the church should be a group of voluntary adults, baptized upon confession of faith, and like the early Christian church, separated from the world and the state.

It began when several young radical students of Zwingli's became disappointed when he pulled back from his earlier

The Anabaptist movement began in 1525 in Zurich, Switzerland at the time of the Protestant Reformation among several of Ulrich Zwingli's students. Zwingli preached at the Grossmünster, pictured above.

stand against baptizing infants. The Reformers were turning their attention to reorganizing society after the religious upheaval; the Anabaptists, led by Conrad Grebel, Georg Blaurock, and Felix Manz, sought a pure church, free from state control (a new and radical idea in those days), open to adult believers from any region.

The movement spread quickly and the Anabaptists were put to death by the thousands; many of the leaders were dead within a few years. This severe persecution often forced the Anabaptists to meet at night. Worship was held secretly, sometimes in caves in the mountains. Leaders travelled illegally, often evading officials to stay alive. This persecution led many to an attitude of withdrawal from the larger society (an attitude still shared by many descendants of the movement today).

The Mennonites

The Anabaptists were not a leaderless group. But they stressed the priesthood of all believers, and because so many of the able leaders were martyred so rapidly, no one leader

This painting by Amish folk artist Aaron Zook depicts the controversy between Mennonite elders Jacob Amman (standing, right) and Hans Reist which led to the beginning of the Amish church in 1693.

emerged. This tradition continues today among the descendant groups.

Perhaps the best known leader was Menno Simons, a Catholic priest from The Netherlands, who joined the movement in 1536. His moderate leadership and prolific writings did so much to unify the scattered Anabaptists that they soon were nicknamed "Mennonites." But Menno shared the leadership with many others.

Today there are Mennonites of many races and tongues in fifty-some countries around the world. Many descend from early beginnings in Switzerland, Germany, and The Netherlands. Many joined the fellowship through mission work. Others sought affiliation at their own initiative.

The Amish

If one believes that the church consists of adults who voluntarily commit themselves to the fellowship and discipline of their fellow believers, then the purity of the church becomes very important.

In 1693, a young Swiss Mennonite elder who felt the church was losing its purity broke with his brethren and formed a new Christian fellowship. His name was Jacob Amman and his followers were nicknamed "Amish." The debate: if a member is excommunicated from the fellowship (the "ban"), how severe should the censure be? Several attempts to heal the division failed.

The Mennonites and the Amish have split many times. Almost always the concern has involved the purity and faithfulness of the fellowship. Personality conflicts have also contributed.

Most Amish groups today consider themselves conservative cousins of the Mennonites. The Old Order Amish live mainly in the United States (22 different states), but some communities are found in the Canadian province of Ontario.

3.

Are they a Christian group or do they represent a different religion?

All Mennonite and Amish groups are devoted to the Christian faith and life. Their tenets and beliefs through the years have essentially paralleled those of other Christians.

Obviously, these people have their own distinctive doctrines and emphases. This has caused many to label them "sectarian," while most modern historians classify them as Protestant denominations. They are not a cult.

Basic beliefs

Attempting to summarize a people's key beliefs is difficult in a short space. Creed and ritual are not important to these groups; in fact, through the years their leaders have warned against confessions of faith replacing the Bible. At various times in history the Mennonites have set down their statement of belief, both for clarity and unity. This first happened only two years after the movement began. A group of Anabaptist leaders met in the Swiss village of Schleitheim and emerged with unanimous conclusions and a spirit of unity which historians agree saved the Anabaptist movement. This "brotherly understanding" is sometimes called the Schleitheim Confession of Faith.

All Amish and Mennonite peoples are Christian groups. In addition to the main tenets of faith and practice accepted by other Christians, they have fostered special emphases on peace and simplicity.

In a word the Mennonites and Amish believe: 1) The one and only God has revealed Himself as existing eternally as Father, Son, and Holy Spirit; 2) The Bible is the authoritative Word of God, and the New Testament is the fulfillment of the Old Testament; 3) God has created and continues to sustain all things; 4) Humankind is sinful, needs atonement through the Lord Jesus Christ, and is free to choose or reject salvation by grace through faith (children are in the kingdom of God until they are old enough to decide); 5) The church is the visible expression of those who voluntarily commit themselves to a life of holiness and love, open to each other's counsel and discipline; and 6) Christ will personally return to judge the world, raise the dead, and usher in the glorious future of the kingdom of God.

Distinctive beliefs

The different groups place varying emphases on these points. The "Old Order," more community-oriented fellowships stress life and practice; the more "modern" groups emphasize the verbal expression of beliefs.

1. From the beginning there has been a strong stress on the separation of church and state. Many historians credit the Anabaptist movement as being the first "free" non-state church.

2. Bible-centeredness pervades all of one's life and faith. The Anabaptists rejected tradition and ritual and emphasized simple obedience to the Word of God. This emphasis continues among the groups today.

3. Probably no teaching has been as dissected by these people as the nature of the church: voluntary, adult, holy, full-time, caring, disciplined.

4. A forgiving love in all of life: this ideal has resulted in most groups through the centuries refusing to participate in war—any war. Peace is a way of life—with one's family,

A favorite story is captured in this etching from the Martyrs Mirror *about Dirk Willems, a Dutch Anabaptist. The sheriff who was pursuing him fell through the ice. Willems helped him to safety, was arrested, and burned at the stake in 1569.*

church members, neighbors, and all human beings every-where in the world.

5. A belief that Christians are different from the world, tra-ditionally called "nonconformity." For some groups it calls for distinctive appearance and mode of transportation; for some it means that a disciple of Christ expresses his beliefs verbal-ly; for some the emphasis falls on ethics and justice.

But universally these groups have believed that Jesus intro-duced a uniquely different approach to the human situation. They live the conviction that the masses of humankind who are not willing to pay the price of Christian discipleship and community sadly miss that unique joy and fulfillment.

4.

Aren't they a bit naive and backward? Why don't they accept modern things?

A New York family (the Smiths), in an air-conditioned Oldsmobile, sits along a Lancaster County road, staring at an Amish father and son (the Fishers) working in a nearby field with two horses and an old piece of equipment which is no longer manufactured.

"It's so peaceful and beautiful," says Mrs. Smith.

"But why do they make it so hard on themselves?" her husband grunts.

"I wish I could live like that," their daughter volunteers.

"No, you don't, darling. You'd go crazy."

"But they look so content, Mom."

Her father pulls that car back onto the road. "It may be nice to look at, Nancy, but you gotta admit it's a little backward."

Few Americans will walk right up to someone else, look them in the eye and say, "Hey, you're pretty backward, aren't you!" But millions like Mr. Smith think such thoughts privately about the Old Order Amish, the Old Order Mennonites, the Hutterites, the Holdeman Mennonites, and other related groups.

What do modern persons (who really intend to be polite and respectful) actually mean when they say "backward?"

In a day when modern progress is running out of steam, an Amish farmer no longer seems so backward and naive. The Old Order communities offer quiet testimony to a viable alternative to modern life.

Is "backward" so bad?

If any of us were to list the five most important things in life—for anyone—what would they be? A sense of meaning. A feeling of personal fulfillment. Having people who really care about us. Having basic necessities—food, shelter, health. And contentment and peace.

Do the Smiths really have a better grip on the essentials of life than the Fishers do?

Does the average modern "progressive" American have a more profound sense of fulfillment and meaning than the Fishers? Do the Smiths actually spend more time with the people who love them than the Fishers do? Is community-centered Amish education truly inferior to Nancy's progressive school? Is the food from the Fisher's garden less healthy than that from the urban supermarket? Do their horses pollute the earth and the air more than the Oldsmobile and its unquenchable demand for gasoline, macadam roads, and parking lots? Will Nancy inherit a better world than the Fisher children?

If modern Americans are not willing to seriously look at these questions, they will have little hope of ever understanding why the Old Order groups have endured for so many generations—and why they are even today growing in number.

The Fishers might ask the Smiths (although most Old Order groups are reluctant to discuss such things with casual strangers), "You say you prefer so-called progress to backwardness. Where will you be when you arrive? Where does this progress take people?"

Progress is running out of steam

As authors we do not wish to treat modern progress unfairly. Certainly great strides "forward" have been made which all peoples everywhere benefit from, especially in the battle against diseases.

These people do not resist progress categorically. The seasons

In an age of scarce resources, decaying environments, dying family structures, extreme loneliness, and disdain for commitments, the Old Order way of life may offer as much fulfillment, meaning, and security as the highly touted "progress" of Western civilization.

themselves have taught them to expect change. But their attitude in an age of scarce resources, decaying environments, dying family structures, extreme loneliness, disdain for commitments, and a high premium on so-called freedoms is "Prove all things; hold fast that which is good." The Old Order communities offer quiet testimony of a viable alternative to modern life.

It should be noted that the majority of Mennonites in North America and around the world have now accepted much of the "modern" dream with most of its trappings. But few are not troubled by the issue in some form or another. In fact, most of the church divisions have focused on matters of how far Christians should go in accommodating modern progress. Many are returning to wood stoves, gardens, more time at home, and simpler lifestyles. But many others find it difficult to sacrifice personal convenience for community fulfillment.

5.

Does anyone ever join them?
Does anyone ever leave?

We know of no group within the highly diverse Mennonite-Amish family which "outsiders" cannot join. The only question is whether the applicant is truly willing to meet the group's requirements of Christian discipleship.

The greater the requirements for membership in the group, the fewer the members who join from the larger society. Conversely, the more relaxed the requirements, the more "outsiders" who join the fellowship (unless the expectations become so low that there's no reason to join).

There's a second side to the joining and leaving story: the children. The "Old Order" groups emphasize keeping their children in the church and grow more because of their own families than "outsiders" who join; more "modern" groups emphasize mission and grow partly because of "outsiders" while their children may feel freer to leave the fellowship.

These are generalizations. There are many exceptions. But they fit the general pattern.

What may a fellowship require?

From the beginning, this question concerned the Mennonites. On this point they broke with the reformers, and the Amish broke from them.

Is it worthwhile to belong to a fellowship where there are no standards of belief and conduct? If the church members

There is no group of Amish or Mennonites anywhere in the world whom an applicant who is truly willing cannot join. Pictured above is a group of youths at a Mennonite church in the south Bronx.

have a right to establish expectations of each other, how are those standards agreed upon, taught, and actually enforced? And should members, who fall short of the standards, be asked to withdraw from membership?

Joining

The Old Order Amish have few modern Americans joining their fellowships. The average American (and the more modern Mennonites) would say it's because the Amish are too strict. An Amish bishop would say most Americans (and many Mennonites) probably aren't willing to submit themselves to the demands of the true Christian way.

Outsiders do join the Old Order groups. One of the leading historians among the Amish of North America is a young man who grew up Catholic, went to Notre Dame University, became acquainted with the Old Order Amish, and later married an Amish girl. This is not a common, everyday happening, but it does happen from time to time. Among the more modern groups, mission activity has accounted for gradual growth.

The Old Order groups are growing much faster than the modern groups. (The Old Order Amish have doubled in membership in the past 20 years!)

The ban and shunning

In a society where freedom of any sort is set on a romantic pedestal, requirements of commitment can appear cruel. To an Old Order person, however, lack of commitment and standards seems cruel and heartless.

The early Anabaptists believed that the New Testament taught the church to discipline its members; that if after long, loving counsel a member in sin refused to repent, that person should be excommunicated from the fellowship until he did repent. Otherwise the fellowship would eventually have no standards.

The purpose of excommunicating a sinful member is to

Belonging to a people is a precious thing. Maintaining that peoplehood requires discipline and sacrifice. Each group draws its boundary lines differently—but no less sincerely.

bring that member back into the fellowship. It is not an attempt to harm or ruin the individual. The actual number of members excommunicated by these groups is very small.

The Old Order Amish vary in their practice of shunning. In its most severe form, members under the ban (excommunication) suffer an almost total shunning from the fellowship. Other members will not eat at the same table with them, do business with them, or visit socially. "But now I have written unto you not to keep company, if any man that is called a brother be a fornicator, or covetous, or an idolater, or a railer, or a drunkard, or an extortioner; with such an one, no, not to eat" (I Corinthians 5:11). But in other communities, shunning may be much more mild.

A sizeable number of persons (primarily young people) do leave the Old Order groups voluntarily, seeking more personal freedom or greater religious piety. Even so, the Old Order Mennonites and Amish are growing rapidly in numbers.

6.

Why do they dress that way?

Peculiar dress patterns seldom start as peculiar dress patterns.

For the Amish and Mennonites who believe that how one lives reflects one's faith, clothing is simply another expression of their deepest convictions. They didn't set out to look odd; they purposed instead to practice humility, simplicity, non-conformity, and modesty.

In the early years of the Anabaptist movement, stress on these principles did not result in a standard form of dress, but in consistently plain and unadorned clothing. Dress reflected contemporary peasant styles. But as these groups' identities began to be threatened by increased interchange with the "world," emphasis on specific modes of dress began to surface. Leaders, sensing a breakdown, began reaching for ways to reinforce their groups' identities.

For many of the groups, dress never became an issue.

But many of the Swiss German groups felt it important to outline specific styles to keep their people separate from the world, nonconformed, and humble.

The Old Order Amish

Men and boys wear dark suit coats which have no lapels and fasten with hooks and eyes. Pants are made in the traditional broadfall pattern and are usually held up by suspenders. Shirts are made of solid colored fabric. Shoes are black for dress up, but often brown for work. Broad-brimmed

These two photos illustrate four different types of prayer veilings ("coverings") worn by various women; also notice the solid dress material and capes of the Amish women in the bottom picture and the less severe capes of the conservative Mennonite woman above.

hats made of either straw or black felt are worn outdoors. The hair is blunt cut and combed front in bangs. Long beards are the mark of an adult man but mustaches are not worn, possibly because of their historical association with the military.

Women and girls wear dresses with full skirts made of solid colored fabric; frequently blue, green, brown, gray, purple or, for some occasions, black. An apron is nearly always worn and a cape often covers the bodice of the dress. Black shoes and stockings are proper for going away.

The women and girls do not cut their hair. They wear it parted in the middle and combed back from the face, then twisted into a bun at the back of the head or nape of the neck. A white, or in some cases black, cap-type head covering is worn in obedience to the Bible passage in I Corinthians 11:2-16. When going out, especially to church, women put on a large black bonnet and shawl. No one wears jewelry.

Old Order Mennonites

Men in these groups do not wear beards and have buttons on their suit coats. Similarly to the Amish, most men wear distinctive plain hats, suit coats without lapels, and suspenders.

Old Order Mennonite women wear modest dresses, often with capes and aprons. Fabric may be in fine prints. White head coverings with tie strings are worn over uncut hair arranged in a bun on the back of the head.

Other Swiss German groups

Most Beachy Amish men still wear suit coats fastened with hooks and eyes, but broadfall pants, suspenders, and plain hats are no longer required in the majority of churches. Beards are often very abbreviated. Most Beachy women wear solid colored dresses with capes. Head coverings usually have tie strings.

Members of conservative Mennonite groups continue to wear the "regulation dress" typical of the Mennonite church

This photo taken at the 1967 Mennonite World Conference in Amsterdam illustrates the wide diversity in appearance practiced by Mennonite women around the world.

during the first half of the 20th century. This includes the lapel-less plain coat worn without a tie for men and a modest cape dress for women. Uncut hair and coverings for women are the rule in these groups and all jewelry is forbidden.

Plain dress was rapidly abandoned in the main body of the Mennonite Church after 1950. Very few members of the largest Mennonite groups wear any kind of distinctive garb. Some continue to maintain standards of simplicity and humility; others have become quite fashion conscious.

7.

Is it true they don't go to war?

Dirk Willems, a Dutch Anabaptist in the late 1560s, was chased by a sheriff who wanted to arrest him because of his faith. Willems crossed the ice of the river safely; the sheriff fell in. Willems went back and helped his persecutor to safety. The sheriff promptly arrested Willems who was then burned at the stake in 1569.

Most Mennonites and Amish refuse to go to war—any war. For four and a half centuries, these people have believed that peaceable, humble Christians will go to prison rather than kill a fellow human being, regardless of nationality or ideology.

Biblical basis

The suffering servanthood of Christ became the model. Leaders taught returning good for evil and turning the other cheek in the name of peace and forgiveness. The courage of New Testament Christians inspired many.

Another favorite story took place in eastern Pennsylvania during the French and Indian war. An Amish settler named Jacob Hochstetler lived in Berks County with his family. But one night a war party of Indians who didn't know Hochstetler attacked his homestead. His sons reached for their guns (used for hunting food) but Jacob threw them out of reach. In what

For four and a half centuries, most of these people have refused to go to war--and have sometimes gone to prison rather than kill a fellow human being. Here two Mennonite leaders testify before Congress.

31

became known as the Hochstetler Massacre, the whole family died except Jacob and his sons, Joseph and Christian, who were carried away by the Indians.

The Mennonites and Amish have stood firmly on their peace position, even when it was painfully unpopular as it was in the two World Wars.

Alternative service

Under the Selective Service, Mennonites and Amish have been able to work for two years in approved alternative service projects in lieu of military service. Conscientious objectors during World War II (forty percent of whom were Mennonites and Amish) worked in hospitals, community service, forestry, or overseas agricultural development and health projects, or were eligible for farm deferments.

Many societies fear people who refuse to go to war. This has resulted in much persecution through the years. In some cases it has resulted in death—an incredible paradox.

A frequent form of service among young people today is Voluntary Service. Young men and women serve varying lengths of time without compensation, with room and board provided at Voluntary Service centers. During the time of the military draft, many young men chose VS for their two years of alternative service. A number of older persons have also joined this servanthood program. There are many related service programs.

Social conscience

Despite their radical stand on war, Amish and Mennonites have generally been regarded as good, solid citizens. They help their neighbors and support community fire and health facilities. They pay their taxes faithfully.

There is also a strong tradition of social conscience among these people. The Mennonites were among the first to protest

Servanthood is more than not going to war. Helping others pervades all of life. Many young people give a year or two to Voluntary Service in teaching, service, and health programs, without pay.

slavery. They continue a strong position against racial and class discrimination.

Among some groups of Mennonites, civil disobedience and protest have become more common. This extends beyond issues of war and race to caring about world hunger and the nuclear danger.

Peace and love in all of life

The Mennonites and Amish seek to express Christian love in all of life. Many have refused to file lawsuits. Participation in labor unions has been cautioned against because of many union practices. Even anger needs to be curbed, they believe.

These people have failed many times in upholding their ideals, yet they have been able to sustain remarkable consistency for centuries.

8.
Why are they against education?

There are two distinct traditions concerning education among the various Amish and Mennonite groups in North America. The majority favor higher education as a good and helpful experience for young people. The minority, including most of the Old Order groups, question whether high school and college lead to greater wisdom and Christian obedience.

Why reject progressive education?

The Old Order Amish are not against education and learning as such. Learning from others is an important value. It is the particular version of education offered by America's consolidated public high schools which especially troubles parents.

An Amish teenager and an average American teenager would probably know about the same number of facts (the Amish child knows less about science, technology, and the arts, but more about soil, animal and plant care, and basic skills like carpentry, masonry and food preservation). In addition the Amish child is bilingual, has an enormous sense of security, and has learned to foster values as a way of life.

The one-room school

Old Order Amish and conservative Mennonite parents want their children to learn basics such as reading, writing,

The Old Order groups are not against education as such. It is the "pro-gressive" education offered by America's consolidated schools which bothers them. They believe school work is only a part of education.

and arithmetic. When these were offered in a local one-room school with a minimum of worldly influences, parents cooperated with the public system. But when schools were consolidated, minimum age requirements raised, and "worldly" courses such as athletics required, these groups developed a strong parochial system of one-room schools.

School for the Old Order groups is only a part of the learning necessary for preparation for the adult world. Work is educational and enjoyable. If a strong agriculture-based community of faith is precious, the schools should reinforce the values basic to that community.

The Old Order Mennonites and Amish pay public school taxes and also pay the full expenses of their parochial system. The landmark 7-0 U. S. Supreme Court decision on May 15, 1972 exempted these and related groups from state compulsory attendance laws beyond the eighth grade. "It is neither

There are dozens of elementary schools, more than 20 high schools, eleven colleges, and three seminaries sponsored directly by Mennonite groups in North America.

fair nor correct to suggest that the Amish are opposed to education beyond the eighth grade level," Chief Justice Burger wrote. "What this record shows is that they are opposed to conventional formal education of the type provided by a certified high school because it comes at the child's crucial adolescent period of religious development."

Many Mennonites promote education

There are dozens of elementary schools, more than 20 high schools, eleven colleges, and three seminaries sponsored directly or indirectly by Mennonite groups in North America.

The majority of Mennonites and some of the more "progressive" Amish groups believe education, either public or private, is a wholesome preparation for life. These private schools generally maintain a high educational standard. They are attended by fewer than half of the people, but are supported financially by most members as a worthwhile religious alternative to the secular school.

Higher education became a vocational necessity as Mennonites left the farm. (The Old Order groups, however, would argue that this trend can be halted by restricting formal education.) Missions and service also gave rise to the need for higher education.

Wisdom

All of these groups believe, as the Bible states, that wisdom and understanding are more important than knowledge and facts. Learning becomes a way of life and leads to respect for all peoples.

9.

Why are they such good farmers?

The Amish and Mennonites have been known as some of the world's best farmers. Not just in the United States but from Russia to Paraguay these people have been found working some of the earth's most productive soil. This resulted from a thorough search for good land and their unusual skills at tilling God's earth.

Love for the land

Few feelings run deeper than an appreciation for soil, especially for a people who have fled from country to country to avoid religious persecution. These people possess a profound sense of stewardship to care for God's creation. Coupled with a belief that work is healthy and enjoyable, these farmers produce plentiful crops by investing long hours and careful planning in their farms.

The typical Lancaster County Amish farm has about 40 acres. Crops include alfalfa, corn, tobacco, and grains. Horses are used in the fields. Steel-wheeled tractors are used only for belt-power to thresh or fill silo. Some of the horse-drawn equipment is very old and is no longer manufactured so Amish craftsmen repair and rebuild it year after year. In some communities, equipment such as hay balers and corn pickers are modern and operated by a gasoline or diesel engine. Studies

The Amish and Mennonites are known as some of the world's best farm-ers. Their profound sense of stewardship, their enjoyment of hard work, and their unusual skills have produced beautiful farms.

Old Order groups often become involved in woodworking or metalworking if they leave the farm; more modern groups enter most other occupations, including the professions, usually with a sense of stewardship and service.

have shown that the Amish farmer produces more harvest per acre with less energy consumption than his neighbor.

Customs vary from community to community. Many Old Order Mennonites do a great deal of their heavy field work with steel-wheeled tractors. More modern Mennonites use the latest and best agri-business equipment available.

Soil represents a wonderful asset to these people. They believe it keeps them close to God. Conservation and new techniques of caring for the soil are taken seriously and are accepted more quickly than a lot of other changes.

The Old Order farm is a home, a place to live and raise one's family, a nearly self-sufficient supermarket on the soil.

Frugality is important and modest profits are plowed back into the land so the next generation will be able to farm, too.

Other occupations

Today a majority of Mennonites in North America are not farmers. Even many Amish sons go to work in cabinet shops or cheese factories because of the scarcity and price of good farmland.

There is virtually no occupation which modern Mennonites do not accept. A few exceptions might be owning a bar or a gambling establishment. But Mennonites can now be found in nearly every profession, including government. Service occupations tend to be favored, however.

The Old Order groups tend to adopt craft-related occupations as they leave the farm, primarily because their caution on education prevents their entering the professions. Some of the finest craftsmanship in cabinets, furniture, and carpentry in Kitchener, Ontario; Goshen, Indiana; Walnut Creek, Ohio; and Lancaster, Pennsylvania are the results of Old Order Mennonite or Amish labor.

Unmarried Old Order women sometimes work away from home doing house cleaning, standing on farmers' markets, or working in a small shop or factory. Many modern Mennonite women are entering the trades or professions, much like their American counterparts.

Food for the world

Mennonites and Amish have always believed strongly in sharing with others from their gardens and their earnings. The Mennonite Central Committee has a very active and innovative worldwide program in relief and agricultural development. Many other church agencies are also dedicated to finding sensitive Christian ways to improve soils and seeds and farming methods in country after country.

10.
Why don't they pay social security taxes?

Although most Mennonites and Amish do not share out of a common purse or live in a "compound," they have the utmost concern for each other's welfare. These people believe that "Bear ye one another's burdens" is a commandment to live by.

Many Old Order Amish believe that if the church is faithful to its calling, many government programs and commercial insurance are not needed. That conviction forced them to testify before Congress because they did not want to receive Social Security benefits. What they wanted instead was the right to look after their own elderly. They were finally given approval, if self-employed, to be exempt from paying the tax. It is rare that an Old Order Amish individual will accept any of the benefits of the Social Security system.

Amish and Mennonites do not object to paying income taxes or real estate, county, and sales taxes. Some of the more "progressive" Mennonites object to paying taxes which go to the federal defense budget.

A cradle-to-grave proposition
Most members of Old Order groups know they are secure for life, no matter if sickness, financial ruin, fire, or old age comes. Their community not only disciplines them; it also supports and restores them.

The Old Order Amish oppose receiving public welfare from the government. Their opposition to the Social Security system was not a reluctance to pay tax; they opposed receiving the benefits of the system.

If someone is widowed or disabled, extended family, neighbors, and church come forward to help with chores and finances for an indefinite period.

Barnraisings are not just social events. They represent help in its most concrete form, not only for their own members, but for neighbors as well.

Grossdadi houses appear as children marry and assume major farming duties. Middle-aged parents move into the new addition, and stay there until their deaths, as active a part of the farm and house operations as their energies allow. When their health deteriorates, help is only steps away on the other side of the house. Meanwhile, three generations live side by side, learning from, advising, looking after each other.

Between 1885 and 1887 the Amish of Lancaster County formed The Amish Aid Fire and Storm Insurance Company to make funds available to members who fall victim to disaster. Still in existence, the Amish Aid Society collects from church members according to their ability to pay. Some other communities have similar plans.

Some Old Order people carry liability insurance from commercial companies on their farms to care for anyone injured on their property. But they do not generally insure commercially for self-protection.

Church insurance companies and retirement villages

Many Mennonites who traffic with the larger world carry comprehensive commercial insurance. But the church and local conferences operate mutual aid programs, inspired by the ethic of brotherhood, that cover the health, cars, and property of their subscribing members.

Most Mennonite communities sponsor their own retirement homes and villages. The commitment is the same—to

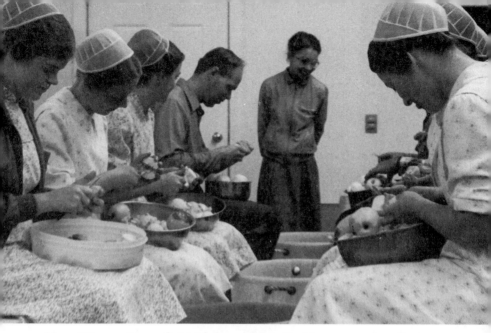

Many Mennonites and Amish become involved in grassroots volunteer efforts to help their neighbors and others around the world. Here a group of Mennonites in Virginia prepare apples for drying.

care for their elderly until death. Usually the church or a quasi-church organization operates these institutions.

Help offered to others, too

But mutual aid is only one part of these people's understanding of caring. Mammoth efforts are directed toward helping others outside their groups. Mennonite Disaster Service is a network of grassroots volunteers—Amish and Mennonite men, women, and youth across North America—who mobilize during national or local disasters to clean up and rebuild. And Mennonite Central Committee sponsors many programs, domestically and overseas, to help others.

11.

Do any of the Amish or Mennonite groups believe in missions?

In 1851 there were Mennonites and related groups in seven countries: the United States, Canada, The Netherlands, Germany, France, Switzerland, and Russia. In 1995 officially organized fellowships of Mennonites and related groups existed in nearly sixty countries around the world.

There is perhaps no more graphic way to underline the results of missionary activity among the Mennonites during the past 150 years. Half of the international fellowship is now nonwhite and lives outside Europe and North America.

The Beachy Amish also have an active mission and service program with congregations in a dozen countries.

The Old Order Amish and the Old Order Mennonite groups and related fellowships do not participate in organized mission outreach as such. They understand their calling to be "missionaries by example" by being the light of the world. Mission work necessitates too many concessions, they reason—giving up farming, distinctive dress, and a separate Christian identity.

Historically a mission church

The early Anabaptists practiced active missionary zeal, going everywhere, preaching and teaching. This contrasted

Many Old Order groups do not participate in organized mission work. They believe in being "missionaries by example." They do support relief programs and projects such as the Fresh Air program.

with the "Christian" society in which they lived where the state magistrate or prince decided the religion of all his subjects. Many Anabaptists died for their faith and their fervor for evangelism.

On August 20, 1527 at Augsburg, Bavaria, a group of Anabaptist leaders met and laid plans for evangelizing the region. Many who were given specific assignments at the conference met their deaths shortly thereafter. Their gathering became known as the "Martyrs Synod."

The Hutterian Brethren were especially zealous among the early Anabaptist groups in their missionary activity.

But as persecution continued to hound the Anabaptists, many sought refuge in the hills and caves and countryside, seeking a stabilized life free of the relentless harassment. The movement settled down, distilling many of the values of the early Anabaptism into a quiet, humble way of life less threatening to authorities. For two and a half centuries, missionary activity virtually ceased as the Mennonites and related groups became known as "the quiet in the land."

A footnote at this point: many Old Order groups today understand themselves as the true and faithful continuation of their conscientious, humble forefathers who for centuries lived their faith as "the quiet in the land." More modern Mennonite and Amish groups, however, view this period of time as their own "dark ages" and reach back to the fiery turmoil and zeal of the early Anabaptism for their sense of faithfulness. There are few gaps in these people's understanding of their own identity which so separate the groups as this one does.

Worldwide mission and service

The first Mennonite missionary since the "settling down" of the movement was sent from The Netherlands to the Dutch East Indies in 1851. The Mennonite Brethren denomination

A hundred years of mission activity by some of the more modern Mennonite groups has resulted in Mennonite and Brethren in Christ fellowships in more than 60 countries around the world. This photo pictures the General Council of the Mennonite World Conference in a meeting in 1993.

was begun in 1860 in Russia by Mennonites who wanted more missionary activity.

Mennonites and Brethren in Christ in North America began domestic mission work in the 1880s. The first foreign missionaries were sent in 1898 and 1899 to India, Turkey, and Southern Rhodesia. Of the main groups in Lancaster County, Pennsylvania, the Lancaster Mennonite Conference launched its mission work in Tanzania in 1934 and the Beachy Amish founded their Amish Mennonite Aid in 1955.

The Mennonites and most Amish groups are quite active in relief and service work. The Mennonite Disaster Service has gained a reliable reputation as a model disaster relief agency. Mennonite Central Committee distributes millions of dollars of service and aid to countries of all political affiliations "in the name of Christ."

12.

What are their weddings like?

When a society's life and future are built on the family, a wedding is an occasion of the greatest joy—and solemnity. Although wedding practices vary greatly among the groups, certain basic assumptions are the same: marriage is for life; divorce and remarriage are simply not considered options; as vital as the bride and groom at a wedding are the attending family and church community, there to give visible support to the new home.

Marriages are not arranged in any of the groups. But neither do they happen in isolation. Especially among the Old Orders, young people meet at the church community's events.

Old Order Amish weddings

For many Old Order Amish, pairing up happens at Sunday evening singings. The young people gather in an appointed barn to sing and visit. A young man takes his girl home and will likely arrange to see her again in another week or two. The couple is secretive about their friendship; in fact, many will not admit to their courtship (although it is known through community grapevines) until they are "published" two days to several weeks before their marriage. In Lancaster County, the "publishing" is done by the deacon. In some other areas, the bishop does this. The wedding and reception are

Marriage is sacred to these people. Commitment is for life. Old Order Amish weddings follow a period of courtship. It is a feast day, a happy time, a solemn occasion for one's family and the community.

held at the bride's home. In many other areas, these functions are held at two different places.

Weddings are held in the bride's home. It will be a feast day. Food and space must be made for two to four hundred guests!

In farming communities life revolves around the seasonal calendar. So in many Pennsylvania settlements, Old Order Amish weddings take place in November when field work is not demanding, usually on Tuesdays and Thursdays. A four-hour service begins the day at 8:30 a.m. It includes wedding hymns from the *Ausbund,* a long sermon on marriage illustrated from the Old Testament, Apocrypha, and New Testament, simple vows (much like many Protestants use), testimonies from church leaders, and an extended prayer.

There are no kisses, rings, photographers, florists, fashion consultants, or caterers. The community conducts the whole affair with careful attention and blessings.

Following the service, cooks serve chicken, filling, mashed potatoes and gravy, ham, relishes, canned fruit, and a host of cakes, pies, and cookies. First to eat are the bride and groom, seated at the *Eck* (corner) table positioned at the choicest spot in the living room. The room is filled twice or three times with guests until all have been fed. A wedding supper, as complete and rich as the dinner, is served, and singing may continue until late in the evening.

The newlyweds do not take a honeymoon. Instead they spend weekends throughout the winter visiting their extended families and receiving wedding gifts. In some cases, the couple does not set up housekeeping until the spring.

Practices vary among other groups

Old Order Mennonite weddings are held in homes, also. But church weddings are the norm for most other groups who traditionally meet in churches. For more "conservative" groups there is austere simplicity—a plain white dress for the bride, perhaps a quartet to sing special music, sometimes a few flow-

This picture depicts the changes being experienced by many Mennonite groups. A "plain" Mennonite grandmother congratulates her grandson and his new wife. Family remains very important.

ers which the bride carries atop a white Bible, no rings.

Among the less "separated" groups, weddings may be complete with gowns, tuxedos, candles, organs, and cascading flowers. The meditation is often short; the usual Protestant vows and wedding music are used.

Among the groups where spouses often meet in college or Voluntary Service, bride and groom frequently plan more personal weddings, combining features from the Old Order services with their own favorite music and perhaps their own personally written vows.

Marriage signals settling down and adopting the responsibilities and expectations of the society. The couple has opted for stability and wisdom.

13.

How are their women and children treated?

An Old Order woman is a worker, a child-bearer, and a companion to her husband, family, and neighbors. She is too busy to participate in a discussion about her own liberation or fulfillment; she would likely prefer to finish painting the hall upstairs, iron the waiting dozen shirts, make soup for the funeral tomorrow, and do a little quilting before the babies wake up and the other children get home from school.

A life of hard work and satisfaction

In a setting where family, church, and community are priorities, personal privacy is almost meaningless. In turn, this woman is unlikely to suffer the modern suburban housewife blues of isolation, worthlessness, and loneliness. She and her farmer husband eat three meals a day together; she has a large family to tend, but they can also share her responsibilities. She is affirmed for the quality of her food, management ability, gardening skills, quilting and sewing gifts.

None of this means that feelings of inadequacy, overwork, and sheer weariness don't threaten to overwhelm these women. But when a woman's ambitions fit her society's framework, and her peers' experiences parallel her own, she is less likely to be restless and dissatisfied.

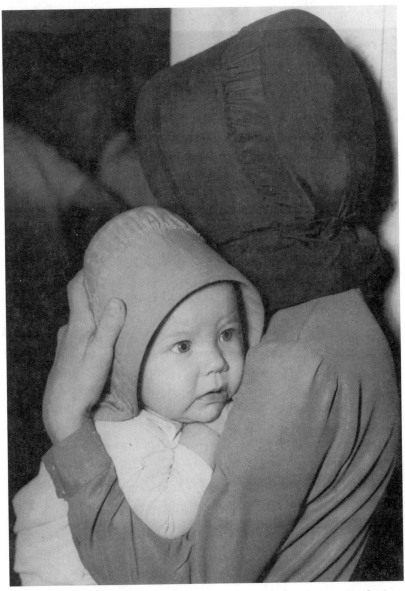

Old Order women have manifold possibilities for socializing. Gardening, food preservation, and quilting usually involve several generations. Then there are auctions, sales, socials, weddings, and endless company.

Relationship to men and children

Among these groups, most farms are co-owned by husband and wife. She will make household purchases, bid at auctions, and write checks to pay the bills.

In church, although not given any leadership, she may participate in congregational votes and nominations for minister, deacon, or bishop. This patriarchal society takes its cues from I Corinthians 11:3, " . . . the head of the woman is the man . . ."

In less traditional groups where women finish high school and many graduate from college, there is still a strong urge to marry and have a family. Increasingly these women develop careers, but often feel a great deal of tension between their jobs and home responsibilities.

Among these more modern groups, women are assuming more church leadership as Sunday school teachers, song leaders, worship leaders, elders. A growing number of Mennonite congregations have ordained women to the ministry. But even here the role of women is often a hot debate.

Children are expected and wanted in the Old Order home. And when they come, they are simply a part of life; their parents experience little trauma of adjustment. For in addition to the completeness a child brings to a home, it makes a wife a mother, her highest priority as a woman in the society, and it adds a worker to the family.

Child-rearing falls primarily to the parents, but few Old Order children grow up in the isolation of a nuclear family. Respect for one's place in the family line is demonstrated in the accurate genealogical lists these people keep in their family Bibles or on folk art renditions on their walls.

From the beginning, Old Order children are rooted in strong structure. They are taught to be disciplined, respectful, and obedient. In this society, age commands respect.

Early on, children are assigned chores. These youngsters work in the company of their parents. Not only do they pick

Children are valued in both the more modern groups as well as in the Old Order groups. Parents work hard to find ways to develop group identity and to pass on faith and values.

up a wide range of skills, but they learn they are a vital part of the family. Their contact with parents, grandparents, brothers, and sisters is close and almost continuous. It is in the fields and the kitchen that the Old Order family is solidified. Active and strong discipline can be handled on the spot by either parents or grandparents.

Moving from the farm

Industry, responsibility, and respect are firm ideals among nearly all groups of Amish and Mennonites. But when the father works away from home, the family lives on an acre or less, and electricity simplifies household chores, major shifts occur in child-rearing.

Some parents belonging to the more modern groups but still hoping to maintain the traditional values look for chores appropriate to their setting. They may plant a stand of raspberry bushes to keep the children busy or help them to find work on weekend farmers' markets.

In the even more assimilated families, children develop their identity by joining the local Little League team or Brownies, or by going to the Y after school until Mom and Dad get home from work.

14.

Is food a part of their religion?

Amish and Mennonites are traditionally great feasters! Most, in this century in North America, have had abundant food available. (There would be two main exceptions: the Depression years when families survived on coffee soup and canned spinach, and World War II when European Mennonite refugees fled to Canada, the American Midwest, and to Central and South Americas, penniless and with empty stomachs.)

Among the many groups in North America, food traditions vary, reflecting the culture of which the people were historically a part. Russian Mennonites prefer vareniky and borscht; the Swiss Germans, scrapple and chicken corn soup; the South Germans, fleisch-kraut and spatzle soup. This chapter will focus on the Swiss German tradition from which most of the Amish and Mennonites of eastern United States and Canada descend.

Food is not a part of our people's faith. But it is a relished part of life. The reasons are clear. Blessed with land and the skills to use it, families garden, butcher, and tend fruit trees with hardly a second thought. Many children make shelling peas, canning applesauce, and pulling corn in massive quantities possible, and convenience food buying impractical. In this setting, a big budget is not needed to eat well. But willingness to devote a lot of time and energy to food preservation and preparation is!

People of the land eat from the land. If one's garden is

People of the land eat from the land. Food is not a part of their faith. But it is a relished part of life, such as this barnraising among Ontario Old Order Mennonites.

Doris Longacre edited the More-with-Less Cookbook *which is "full of suggestions by Mennonites on how to eat better and consume less of the world's limited food resources."*

bountiful, so is one's table. And so menus reflect the seasons, the soil, and the climate.

You will find Amish and Mennonite women's recipe files and family cookbooks heavy on desserts, pickles, and jams, and light on vegetables, salads, and meats. That means two things—the challenge and delight in cooking for these women of Swiss German background came in exploring infinite varieties of pies, cakes, and puddings; vegetables, salads, and meats are best prepared in rather standard form.

Corn, peas, lima beans, and green beans are at their best, reason these people, when handled simply—steamed until tender, then salted and bathed in brown butter. No recipes are needed for that. This is a generalization, of course.

Menus reflect seasons

Little experimenting has been done with salads. The tossed variety appears on tables when gardens run over with lettuce and tomatoes. Traditional cooks seem to prefer molded salads, calling for canned or less perishable vegetables like carrots and cabbage, or salad "substitutes"—chow-chow, pickles, and cole slaw. The pickled dishes reflect the seasonal approach to cooking. In the absence of freezers, preserving has been done in arch cellars, springhouses, and pickling brines.

Butchering and meat preparation, like gardening, have been almost an impulse of the culture. Traditionally one could tell the season by the meat served. A choice pig and steer, butchered in December or January, made fresh meat available those months with smoked and cured hams, bacon, bologna, sausage, and canned steaks for the rest of the year. The farm's chickens and fish from the stream rounded out the meat menu.

Bushels of fruit are canned each summer, providing the family with a year of beauty, sweetness, and vitamins, until fresh fruit again ripens.

More-with-less

Swiss and German food preferences can be traced in these diets. The food is rich and heavy with carbohydrates and fats. Knepp, rivels, dumplings, butter, and cream are digestible fare for physically active farmers. But weight problems and overeating threaten. The more sedentary lifestyle that comes with professional careers has begun to alter some of these people's eating patterns. So has an increased awareness of the world's food needs.

A useful tool in applying the heritage of gardening, canning, and drying foods, and the ability to cook with whatever is at hand, is the *More-with-Less Cookbook*. Published in 1976 by Herald Press, the Mennonite Church publishing house, the cookbook is full of "suggestions by Mennonites on how to eat better and consume less of the world's limited food resources."

15.

Do they go to doctors and hospitals?

Most Mennonite and Amish groups do not oppose modern medicine. They go to doctors, take pills and medicines, and enter the hospital when necessary.

In fact, because of the opportunities for service, medicine and health care have traditionally been among the first professions entered by persons who leave the farm and get higher learning.

Biblical understanding of healing

Like most Christians, these people believe that healing is a gift from God. "The Lord gives and the Lord takes away." This is not a rejection of modern medicine; it is simply acceptance of the fact that after one has done all that is humanly possible, one must leave all in God's hands.

The Old Order caution

The Old Order Amish and Old Order Mennonites are often portrayed in the national press as opposing modern medicine. This is not true. There is nothing in their religious teaching against the use of doctors, medicine, or hospitals.

During a 1979 outbreak of polio in Pennsylvania among unimmunized persons, including several Amish victims, a

Most Mennonites and Amish do not oppose modern medicine. They go to doctors, take pills and medicines, and enter the hospital when necessary.

reputable Philadelphia newspaper ran a front-page story declaring that this was only the second time in history when Old Order Amish agreed to receive modern medicine. This is grossly untrue.

Most Old Order families will seek a doctor's advice and enter the hospital if necessary. Faith healing as such has never been much of a movement among the Amish and Mennonites.

Home remedies do receive a lot of attention from Old Order persons. This is not unlike other rural peoples who believe good food, honey, tea, and vinegar may do as much for good health as drugs. Traces of superstition do exist. Some members travel to non-medical clinics scattered across the country; others visit mines and springs on the recommendation of family and friends who have found help. Chiropractors also enjoy a large following among these groups. But the Old Order religious communities stand out in stark contrast to the overdrugged, legislation-happy society of the modern age.

When Old Order leaders express caution to government health programs, observers need to remember how often the government has confronted these people with laws and rulings which violate their beliefs (compulsory school attendance, Social Security benefits, the military draft, etc.).

Humanitarian mission

Mennonite groups have begun and continue to operate many health facilities throughout North America. Mennonite doctors and nurses are dedicated to serving anyone who needs care.

An irony of their history is that many Mennonite health institutions were begun or expanded as a result of the military draft. Young men seeking alternative service often found work in health facilities.

When Old Order leaders express caution to government health programs, observers need to remember how often the government has confronted these people with laws and rulings which violate their beliefs.

Mental health

Mennonites and Amish probably have about as much mental illness as the larger society. The teachings on humility and perfection tend to exert pressure on the individual. Suicide is thought by some experts to be as common as among the general American culture.

On the other hand, the sense of belonging and community often add a sense of togetherness and peace of mind.

A gift from God

These people believe that good health, both physical and mental, is a gift from God and requires careful stewardship on the part of the individual. And they believe their Christian calling inspires them to reach out and minister to the needs of others as they are able.

16.

What about burial?

In a close community, grief is often shared by everyone. Death is a time for embrace; family, friends, and neighbors gather quietly without hysteria. For rural farm people with a sense of life's rhythms, death is accepted as the inevitable.

Simplicity in death

There is little flurry in the Old Order Amish community about funeral, burial, and estate plans. Custom provides for style of coffin, clothing, and the funeral service itself; the church and family stand by with financial help if needed.

Funeral and burial usually take place three days after death. During those days the community visits the family to offer sympathy and help.

A funeral director from the local area assists in a minimal way which usually includes embalming, and sometimes includes supplying the coffin and the hearse.

In death, as in life, simplicity is the order. A plain wooden coffin is built. Frequently it is six-sided with a split lid; the upper part being hinged so it can be opened for viewing the body. Ornate carving, finely grained wood, and delicate fabrics have no place here.

These people seldom lose sight of their place in the universe. And their funerals—basic, solemn, hopeful—are testament to that understanding.

In many communities, the body is traditionally dressed in

66

Even children learn that death is a part of life's rhythms (bottom); above, a young Mennonite Brethren couple stands by their young daughter's coffin which they had their close church friends build as part of their grief-love. Grief in community is often less lonely.

The tone of an Amish funeral is hopeful, yet full of admonition for the living. There are no eulogies. Respect for the deceased is expressed, but not praise. A hymn is spoken, but not sung.

white. When the body has been prepared for burial, it is brought home again where it will be viewed and the funeral held. Family and friends gather around the coffin for the nearly two hour service. The tone of an Amish funeral is hopeful, yet full of admonition for the living. There are no eulogies. Respect for the deceased is expressed, but not praise. A hymn is spoken, but not sung.

Burial usually takes place in a hand-dug grave in a church district cemetery. No flowers are placed there, only a simple tombstone to mark the spot, much like all the rest surrounding it. As in life, one individual is not elevated above another.

Following the burial, family, friends, and neighbors eat together to help the bereaved return to routine and normal life again. The family can relax in the relationships that remain.

Burial among other groups

The same attitudes of hope, shared grief, and humility prevail among other Amish and Mennonites as well. Specific practices differ, but in most cases the tone is the same.

Many Old Order Mennonite groups hold a short funeral service at home for the family. A viewing is held outside the meetinghouse before the main service, followed by the burial. Then the funeral service takes place in the meetinghouse for the gathered communtiy.

Other groups who worship in church buildings will hold their funerals in the church, three days following death. A meditations, full of hope yet instruction for the living, is given; there is a lot of singing about the comfort and joy of the next world.

Caskets tend to be simple although not usually handmade; the body is dressed in the person's best clothes, but not specially designed ones.

Burial most often takes place in a cemetery adjoining the church, following a short graveside service. More individuality is shown in the choice of tombstones among less traditional groups.

An increasing number of families from more progressive groups are trying to capture the community and simplicity that has surrounded Old Order funerals. Family members may build the coffin, dig the grave, dress the body, and plan a very personal memorial service. Their focus is directed away from the industry's trappings and toward the need for embrace from church and friends.

17.

Don't they believe in having fun?

Most Old Order people are proof alive that it is possible to have fun without a TV, a wind-up toy, a well-proportioned doll, and golf clubs. Here are people who manage to enjoy life without the assistance of the entertainment industry.

That doesn't mean they feel deprived, self-sacrificing, or are against fun. They just make their own. Visiting or playing ball or going to a sale comes as reward at the end of a long work day or week. The rest of the time, fun happens as one works—good stories while canning peaches, daring one's brothers while stacking hay on the wagon, throwing rotten tomatoes.

Homemade fun

Old Order children have toys—some bought, some homemade, a lot of them hand-me-downs. But what's more, these children have playmates—their own brothers and sisters plus a host of cousins and neighbors. And recreation for adults is almost always group centered.

These people are serious about life, and practice an austere and disciplined lifestyle. That does not generally make them unpleasant or grim. It does mean that grown-ups, especially, may be cautious about indulging too much time in play. For most of the groups, from Old Order to modern, work is hon-

These people, though serious and almost austere, do enjoy life. Recreation for adults is usually group centered. Children have toys, some bought, some homemade, and a lot of hand-me-downs. Playing together is a high point of community life.

Play among children in community fosters more creativity and less competition. Children learn how to visit, how to work together, and how to tell stories.

orable; recreation is somewhat suspect; guilt rises up when they think they're having "too much" fun.

Farm life offers its own diversions: swimming in the creek, playing ball after supper, building tunnels in the haymow, sewing new doll clothes, riding bike to the neighbors. Large families make possible good baseball or basketball games, lively table games (from Rook to Monopoly), boisterous sledding and ice skating, and endless debates and discussions while doing the milking or while washing dishes.

These people are great visitors and rich storytellers. Family reunions are summer highlights. Sunday afternoons are meant for calling on friends, neighbors, and family. Quiltings become all-day visits, structured, of course, around productive efforts and a lot of food.

Sunday evening church, youth group meetings, and summer and winter Bible Schools are anticipated social events among more "conservative" Mennonite groups.

Horse and livestock auctions, although attended for serious business reasons, are outings for the farmer. And few men and women can pass up a public household sale in the neighborhood if farm and housework permit.

Music and reading

Young people gather often around music: for many Old Order Amish, the occasions are singings, barn games, and hoedowns; many "conservative" Mennonite youth join a chorus with weekly practice sessions and Sunday evening programs. More modern groups will top off a weekend retreat or a gathering of friends with a cappella singing from their church's hymnbook.

In the more traditional homes, books are at a premium. There are few novels and almost no modern nonfiction. The Bible is there, some Bible storybooks for children, and most likely *The Martyrs Mirror,* Menno Simons' writings, and a few prayer and inspirational books. Old Order groups often subscribe to the local daily paper and frequently to *The Budget,* a weekly newspaper with correspondents from Amish communities across North America. Many also read the monthly inspirational magazines from Pathway, an Old Order Amish publishing house in Aylmer, Ontario.

Among the groups where education is more of a priority, books and magazines often abound. Here entertainment patterns as a whole differ. Members have television, church youth groups go roller skating, dates attend movies, families own campers. Yet even so, a deep respect for work usually remains, and one's most precious moments of fun are often with one's family.

18.

What are some
of their problems?

Many people find the Mennonite-Amish family enchanting, but as they observe more closely, become disappointed with their weaknesses and inconsistencies. Sometimes this results in harsh, sweeping criticisms.

Our purpose here is to pinpoint some of the most nagging problems of the various groups. Not all members will agree with our analysis. But it seems fair to attempt a charitable but straightforward answer to this question.

Most closely-knit groups tend to be very sensitive to criticism from either inside the group or outside. Mennonites and Amish generally fit this pattern. However, most of the fellowships offset this supersensitivity by stressing humility in all things.

The perfect people

Jesus said: "Be ye therefore perfect as I am perfect."

As often happens when people attempt to be as Christ-like, consistent, and perfect as possible, several results surface again and again among the various Amish and Mennonite groups: 1) a beautiful Christian community takes root and thrives as a living example of redeemed humankind; 2) the dual themes of perfection and humility provide fertile milieu for many, but tear other persons apart; 3) those who can't stand the tension suffer emotional and spiritual anguish.

A vivid illustration of a nagging problem of a people seeking perfection: these three Mennonite churches lie within a mile of each other in a small Pennsylvania village; the first group wanted more organization and education; the second group resisted the introduction of the Sunday school, the use of the pulpit, and the English language in worship.

One of the ironies of these people: as careful stewards of the earth, they have become wealthy landowners. This affluence threatens both their way of life and their faith.

Those in anguish take several approaches: a) denial of their feelings, resulting in unhappiness and even mental illness; b) more commonly, they leave the group, either to form a new "perfect" community, or to become more flamboyant and join the mainstream "imperfect" society.

This stress on the Christian virtues of perfection and humility has been both one of the greatest assets and one of the greatest weaknesses of the Mennonites and Amish. It has brought into being some of the most unusual and beautiful Christian communities in all history; it has also resulted in dozens of church splits, self-righteousness, and unhealthy rebellion and rejection.

Affluence

If one were to poll leaders within the worldwide peoplehood and ask for their single most corrosive problem, the

76

near-unanimous verdict would be affluence.

It may seem strange for a people with a long history of persecution and migrations to fear settledness, peace, and enough food. The problem for those who live in Europe and North America, however, is that there is more than enough.

The Old Order peoples see wealth as an allurement from the self-denying life to join the worldly indulgent society. For modern-appearing but community-oriented Mennonite groups, affluence is viewed as the force that leads to war and famine because it makes all humans greedy. And even the more modern groups can't escape the nagging conscience, born of centuries of suffering and discipleship, that the overstuffed of the world are unlikely to be Christ's servants.

Inside or outside

Are Christians called to be prophets or benevolent kings? This tension underlines many of the current discussions among the various groups: "To what extent do we join the world?"

The Dutch Mennonite groups have a stronger tradition of participating in the establishment of their societies while seeing themselves as the salt of the earth; most of the Swiss Mennonites and the Amish, however, have expressed extreme caution on governmental involvement. "How can one serve in government but refuse to go to war?" might be a typical question.

At the core of this discussion lies the central issue: do they want to continue to be a distinguishable Christian people?

In summary

Many other problems could be highlighted, such as the tension between the group and the individual. But these have been broad strokes. Thousands of pages of history books document these generalities with specific stories and illustrations from one community after another.

19.

Are they growing or dying in number?

Most of the groups around the world which make up the diverse Mennonite-Amish family are growing in number. The fastest growing bodies are Mennonites in several African countries and in Indonesia and India. The only group losing significant numbers is one which has traditionally been among the largest and the most "liberal," the Dutch Mennonite Brotherhood in The Netherlands.

Statistics from Mennonite World Conference list the worldwide baptized membership of all the groups in 1994 as 973,991. More than half of the members now live outside North America and Europe.

The fastest growing groups in North America tend to be the Old Order groups: the Old Order Amish, the Hutterian Brethren, the Old Order Mennonites, and the Beachy Amish. Using the definitions we introduced in Chapter 1 of the "Old Order" groups and the "modern" groups, one can surmise from the statistics that about 40% of the groups in North America are Old Order in their approach to life and faith. (The Old Order Amish have doubled in population in the past 20 years.)

Membership (excluding children who are not yet communicant members) in the main bodies of Mennonite-related groups in North America are as follows:

An historic moment: six Mennonite leaders, one from each continent, officiated at the mass communion service at the 10th Mennonite World Conference in Wichita, Kansas, during July 1978. There are organized conferences and bodies of Mennonite-related groups in more than 60 countries with a total 1994 membership of 973,991.

Mennonite Church (MC) (only)	84,092
Old Order Amish	65,250
General Conference Mennonite Church (GC) (only)	51,794
General Conference of Mennonite Brethren Churches	45,202
MC—GC dual-affiliated	24,448
Brethren in Christ General Conference	20,829
Conservative Mennonite movement (several groups)	17,250
Hutterian Brethren	14,000
Church of God in Christ Mennonite (Holdeman)	13,740
Old Order Mennonite (buggy)	10,000
Conservative Mennonite Conference	8,978
Beachy Amish Mennonite	7,089
Old Order Mennonite (car)	6,500
Evangelical Mennonite Conference	6,260
Old Colony Mennonite Church	5,200
Fellowship of Evangelical Bible Churches	4,380
Sommerfeld Mennonite Church of Manitoba	4,245
Evangelical Mennonite Church	4,059
Evangelical Mennonite Mission Conference	3,476
Chortitzer Mennonite Conference	1,539
Sommerfeld Mennonites of Saskatchewan and Alberta, et al.	1,500
Mennonite Christian Fellowship	1,145
Bergthaler Mennonite Churches of Saskatchewan and Alberta	1,010

Society of Brothers	998
Independent Amish Mennonites (Kauffman)	900
United Zion Church	861
Reinlander Mennonite Church	850
New Reinland Mennonite Church	613
Charity Christian Fellowship	500
Reformed Mennonite Church	412
Kleine Gemeinde Mennonite	412
Old Order River Brethren	319
Unaffiliated Amish Mennonites of Tennessee and Kentucky	300
Zion Mennonite Church	300
Emmanuel Mennonite Church	200

The main groups in Lancaster County, Pennsylvania, are as follows (listed with 1995 estimates of the number of their baptized members who attend congregations located in Lancaster County):

	# of Congreg- ations	Members
Lancaster Mennonite Conference (MC)	(87)	11,945
Old Order Amish	(105)	8,000
Brethren in Christ	(18)	3,210
Old Order Mennonite (buggy)	(10)	2,585
Old Order Mennonites (car)	(12)	2,512
Atlantic Coast Mennonite Conference (MC)	(9)	2,033
Beachy and other Amish Mennonite churches	(9)	960
Eastern Pennsylvania Mennonite Church	(10)	958
United Zion Church	(8)	652
Dual-affiliated General Conference/ Atlantic Coast Conference Mennonite	(2)	508
General Conference Mennonite	(3)	485
Mid-Atlantic Mennonite Fellowship	(5)	427
Unaffiliated Mennonite	(7)	410
Stauffer and related Mennonite churches	(4)	350
Reidenbach Mennonite	(8)	200
New Order Amish	(2)	150
Old Order River Brethren	(2)	96
Hope Mennonite Fellowship	(1)	75
Reformed Mennonite	(1)	68
Fellowship churches	(1)	67
United Mennonite	(1)	10

All told, these many groups total 35,701 in membership and with their families account for about 15% of the population of Lancaster County. Each group has its own interpretations of various teachings, along with given attitudes toward dress, transportation, education, leadership, peace and justice, and evangelism. These interpretations and standards of faith and life continue to change and evolve in each of the groups from year to year. Some groups, such as Lancaster Mennonite Conference (which is the largest conference of the largest Mennonite body in the world), maintain a great deal of diversity of practice within their fellowships; some others, such as the Old Order (Pike) Mennonites, permit little diversity.

Lancaster County is the largest Mennonite community in the world. Winnipeg, Manitoba, is the second largest.

Lancaster County is the second largest Amish community in the world. Holmes County, Ohio, is the largest.

One of the most important conversations in recent years has been between Mennonite women. Here at a Mennonite World Conference gathering in Bulawayo, Zimbabwe, are Inneke Reinhold-Scheuermann (left), pastor from The Netherlands, Margaret Awartey (center), from Ghana, and Leonor de Méndez (right), pastor from Guatemala.

Mennonite and Brethren in Christ World Membership

Areas	Country	Membership
Africa		
	Angola	2,600
	Burkina Faso	63
	Ethiopia	50,018
	Ghana	1,500
	Kenya	11,682
	Malawi	240
	Mozambique	22,900
	Nigeria	7,251
	South Africa	199
	Tanzania	19,486
	Zaire	136,200
	Zambia	8,362
	Zimbabwe	16,152
	Total	**276,653**
Asia & Australia		
	Australia	40
	Hong Kong	94
	India	84,195
	Indonesia	60,709
	Japan	3,460
	Philippines	1,059
	Taiwan	1,400
	Vietnam	100
	Total	**151,057**
Caribbean, Central & South America		
	Antigua and Barbados	795
	Argentina	2,885
	Belize	2,429
	Bolivia	6,664
	Brazil	5,974
	Colombia	2,134
	Costa Rica	1,725
	Cuba	45
	Dominican Republic	2,163
	Ecuador	213
	El Salvador	262
	Guatemala	3,971

	Haiti	901
	Honduras	9,841
	Jamaica	505
	Mexico	20,478
	Nicaragua	5,093
	Panama	710
	Paraguay	22,512
	Peru	323
	Puerto Rico	596
	Trinidad and Tobago	86
	Uruguay	887
	Venezuela	244
	Total	**91,436**
Europe		
	Austria	350
	Belgium	85
	Commonwealth of Independent States	3,350
	France	2,000
	Germany	24,414
	Great Britain	88
	Ireland	6
	Italy	160
	Luxembourg	100
	Netherlands	15,500
	Portugal	14
	Spain	265
	Switzerland	2,800
	Total	**49,132**
North America		
	Canada	117,932
	United States	287,781
	Total	**405,713**
Summary		
	Africa	276,653
	Asia & Australia	151,057
	Caribbean, Central & South America	91,436
	Europe	49,132
	North America	405,713
	Total	**973,991**

20.

What, in fact, holds them together?

These people believe God has called them to a life of faith, dedication, humility, and service. It is that belief in God's personal interest in their lives and their communities which holds them together, in spite of many forces which could easily pull them apart.

This truth cannot be overstressed.

Without a strong belief in God and the seriousness of life, these people as a people would have disappeared many decades ago.

The Old Order unity

One can observe many paradoxes about the Old Order way of life. An outsider describes the Old Order communities as though they were prisons from which the people yearn to flee; an Amish farmer marvels at the lostness of the larger society as they rush about without families, without faith and tradition, without peace. Each pities the other!

The Old Order communities offer a visible alternative to modern life. There is no other way to explain why so many tens of thousands stay, why in fact the communities are growing in number, why the whole world is fascinated by the qual-

These peoples' belief in God has sustained them throughout the centuries. The entire world is fascinated by the quality of the human wholeness they sense in the faces and the fields of these people.

Menno Simons' favorite verse was I Corinthians 3:11 which continues as a watchword for these people: "For other foundation can no one lay than that is laid, which is Jesus Christ."

ity of human wholeness they sense in the faces and fields of these people. The joy and security a child experiences from true peoplehood is a gift most children in today's world never have an opportunity to know.

We do not wish to romanticize. The Old Order communities have their problems and weaknesses. But their strengths must far outweigh their failings, if we are to believe the evidence. Most of the communes, which took root in the 60s all across the United States, did not last twelve months. How about centuries? We believe such an endeavor takes a central faith, courage and discipline, and a wonderfulness which overcomes the world.

The Old Order world is not paradise; neither is it hell. It is perhaps one of the most meaningful and unusual approaches to human life in modern history. A people of God. A people apart. A people together.

Cohesiveness among more modern groups

Several main unities can be observed among the more modern groups. Some stress evangelical faith as the distinguishing characteristic of their group. Some seek new symbols of service and artistic expression. Some emphasize radical peace and social concerns as the unity binding them together. All of these understandings are currently effective in holding together large, diverse bodies of more modern Mennonites.

It is perhaps instructive to note that the fastest growing groups among the whole worldwide Mennonite-Amish peoplehood are the first-generation believers in Africa, Asia, and Latin America, and the Old Order "settled" groups of North America. Those Mennonites for whom the first generation is four and a half centuries ago and for whom the discipline of the "settled-down" peoplehood is also something of the past are unsure of their identity. Many of them will disappear into the mainstream society, both in faith and lifestyle.

To follow Christ truly

We close this book with three favorite quotations of many of our people:

"What does the Lord require of you, but to do justly, and to love mercy, and to walk humbly with your God." (Micah 6:8)

"For other foundation can no one lay than that is laid, which is Jesus Christ." (Menno Simon's favorite verse from I Corinthians 3:11)

"No one can truly know Christ except to follow him in life." (Testimony of Anabaptist leader Hans Denk)

Glossary

ALTERNATIVE SERVICE—Various service projects administered by the church which fulfilled government draft obligations, yet did not violate church members' peace positions.

AMISH AID SOCIETY—An organization built on the principle of mutual aid. Church members pay annually into a reserve fund that is then available when disaster strikes a member.

ANABAPTIST—The nickname meaning "rebaptizer," given to the radical group of "Brethren" during the Protestant Reformation who advocated adult baptism. They believed the church should be a group of voluntary adults, baptized upon confession of faith.

AUSBUND—The hymnal used by most Old Order Amish, first published in Europe in 1564. It is a collection of lyrics and verses only; tunes are not printed but are transmitted orally.

BAN—The practice of excommunication used as a means of keeping the church pure. The ban, based on I Corinthians 5:11, takes many forms, from members being refused communion to having other members not eat with them, visit, or do business with them. One of the issues over which the Amish and Mennonites split in 1693. The practice is designed to bring a member back into fellowship.

BARNRAISING—The practice of rebuilding with volunteer labor a barn that has been destroyed. Amish and Mennonite men gather for a day of work and socializing to build the bulk of the structure. The women generally provide a large meal.

BISHOP—An ordained overseer of several congregations within a church district. His role is to coordinate leadership and decisionmaking, as well as to officiate at communion, weddings, and funerals.

BROADFALL TROUSERS—A style of trousers worn by many Old Order Amish men which has, instead of a front zipper, a broad flap of cloth that is buttoned shut.

BUDGET (THE)—A weekly paper which carries news of Old Order Amish communities across North America. Through its regular correspondents, it serves as an effective contact among the scattered groups.

BUGGY—The horse-drawn carriage used for transportation by many Old Order Amish and some Old Order Mennonites. Although specific styles vary from community to community, buggies reflect a common commitment to simplicity and suspicion toward technology held by those who use them.

CAPE—An additional piece of material which fits over the bodice of a dress. Worn by most Older Order and many "conservative" women, it is designed for modesty.

ECK—The special corner table in the living room where the Old Order Amish bridal party sits to eat following the wedding.

GROSSDADI HOUSE—The extension added to a home when a married child takes over the farm. Parents move into the new smaller section; the young, growing family occupies the large original part.

MARTYRS MIRROR—The large book of stories of Anabaptist martyrs, originally published in 1660. Full of graphic accounts of Christians dying for their faith, a copy is found in most Old Order homes and many modern ones.

MARTYRS SYNOD—The gathering of early Anabaptists (1527) who laid plans for evangelizing Bavaria. Many were killed as they carried out their commissions.

MENNONITE CENTRAL COMMITTEE—The inter-Mennonite relief organization that supplies food, clothing, community development workers, and financial aid overseas and throughout North America.

MENNONITE DISASTER SERVICE—A network of grassroots volunteers—Mennonite and Amish men, women, and youth—across North America who mobilize during national or local disasters to clean up and rebuild.

MODERN—A descriptive term used by the authors to designate those among the Mennonites and Amish who are more influenced in their primary decisionmaking by what the larger society thinks than by what their faith fellowship believes.

NONCONFORMITY—A belief that Christians are different from the world. Amish and Mennonite groups have given the concept expression in a variety of ways—distinctive dress styles, modes of transportation, wariness toward technology, living peaceably with all, advocating justice, and the ethic of love.

NONRESISTANCE—Love in practice; the ideal of returning good for evil, taught by Christ. Its practical expression means refusing to participate in any war, protesting class and racial discrimination, and, for some, protesting nuclear danger and world hunger. It is a peaceful approach to life that has also meant, for many, refusing to file lawsuits, participate in labor unions, or express excessive anger.

OLD ORDER—A descriptive term used by the authors to designate those among the Amish and Mennonites who take their cues for decisionmaking primarily from their faith fellowship (instead of the larger world).

PATHWAY PUBLISHERS—An Old Order Amish publishing house in Aylmer, Ontario, that publishes three monthly inspirational magazines—*Family Life, Young Companion,* and *Blackboard Bulletin.* In addition, they publish schoolbooks (for Old Order schools), story books, adult instructional books, cookbooks, and some historical books in German.

PRAYER VEILING—The head covering worn by women when "praying or prophesying": an interpretation of I Corinthians 11.

"PRIESTHOOD OF ALL BELIEVERS"—The Biblical concept that within the church each member is responsible to counsel, discipline, and support all other members. Although leaders are believed to be ordained of God, they are selected from the laity and act as servants of the church.

"PUBLISHED"—The announcing of an Amish couple's plans to marry. The announcement is made by a bishop during a Sunday morning service.

"THE QUIET IN THE LAND"—Name given to Anabaptist groups as the movement settled down and many members fled to rural areas.

SCHLEITHEIM CONFESSION OF FAITH—The agreement arrived at by divergent Anabaptist groups scattered across Europe in 1527. It is often credited with unifying the fellowships sufficiently to save the movement.

SHUNNING—An expression of the ban in which members do not keep company with an offending member who has fallen out of fellowship. Varies from community to community.

SINGING—A gathering of Old Order Amish young people for socializing, singing together, and playing games.

STEEL-WHEELED TRACTORS—Used by some Old Order farmers for field work. The steel wheels remove the temptation to use the tractor for transportation on the road.

VOLUNTARY SERVICE—Church-administered projects which allow members to offer from three months to two years of their time for service overseas or at home, without pay.

Bibliography

Amish Cooking. Pathway Publishers, Aylmer, ON, 1965.

Arnold, Eberhard. *Children's Education in Community.* The Plough Publishing House, Rifton, NY, 1976.

Bender, H.S. *Anabaptist Vision.* Herald Press, Scottdale, PA, 1955.

Braght, Thieleman J. van. *Martyrs Mirror.* Herald Press, Scottdale, PA, 1938.

Brown, Hubert L. *Black and Mennonite.* Herald Press, Scottdale, PA, 1976.

Burkholder, J.R. and Calvin Redekop, ed. *Kingdom, Cross and Community.* Herald Press, Scottdale, PA, 1976.

DeAngeli, Marguerite. *Henner's Lydia.* Doubleday, New York, NY, 1937.

_____. *Yonie Wondernose.* Doubleday, New York, NY, 1944.

Denlinger, A. Martha. *Real People.* Herald Press, Scottdale, PA, 1993.

Detweiler, Richard C. *Mennonite Statements on Peace.* Herald Press, Scottdale, PA, 1968.

Devoted Christian's Prayer Book, A. Pathway Publishers, Aylmer, ON, 1967.

Drescher-Lehman, Sandra. *Meditations for New Moms.* Good Books, Intercourse, PA, 1994.

Dyck, Arnold. *Lost in the Steppe.* Henry D. Dyck, trans. Derksen Printers, Steinbach, MB, 1974.

Dyck, Cornelius J. *An Introduction to Mennonite History.* Herald Press, Scottdale, PA, 1993.

_____. *Twelve Becoming.* Faith and Life Press, Newton, KS, 1973.

Epp, Frank H. *Mennonite Exodus.* D.W. Friesen, Altona, MB, 1962.

_____. *Mennonites in Canada 1786-1920: The History of a Separate People.* Macmillan, New York, NY, 1974.

_____. *Mennonites in Canada, 1920-1940.* Macmillan, Toronto, ON, 1982.

Family Life. Amish periodical published monthly. Pathway Publishers, Aylmer, ON.

Fisher, Gideon L. *Farm Life and Its Changes.* Pequea Publishers, Gordonville, PA, 1978.

Fisher, Sara E. and Rachel K. Stahl. *The Amish School.* Good Books, Intercourse, PA, 1986.

Funk, Joseph and Sons. *The Harmonia Sacra, Twenty-fifth Edition.* Good Books, Intercourse, PA, 1993.

Gingerich, Melvin. *Mennonite Attire Through the Centuries.* Pennsylvania German Society, Breinigsville, PA, 1970.

Gingerich, Orland. *The Amish of Canada.* Herald Press, Scottdale, PA, 1973.

Glick, Aaron S. *The Fortunate Years: An Amish Life.* Good Books, Intercourse, PA, 1994.

Good, Merle. *Going Places.* Good Books, Intercourse, PA, 1994.

_____. *Hazel's People.* Herald Press, Scottdale, PA, 1971.

_____. *Today Pop Goes Home.* Good Books, Intercourse, PA, 1993.

_____. *Who Are the Amish?* Good Books, Intercourse, PA, 1985.

Good, Merle and P. Buckley Moss. *Reuben and the Fire.* Good Books, Intercourse, PA, 1993.

_____. *Reuben and the Blizzard.* Good Books, Intercourse, PA, 1995.

Good, Phyllis Pellman. *The Best of Amish Cooking.* Good Books, Intercourse, PA, 1988.

_____. *A Mennonite Woman's Life: Photographs by Ruth Hershey (1895-1990).* Good Books, Intercourse, PA, 1993.

Good, Phyllis Pellman, Kate Good and Rebecca Good. *Amish Cooking for Kids.* Good Books, Intercourse, PA, 1995.

Good, Phyllis Pellman and Merle Good. *Ideas for Families.* Good Books, Intercourse, PA, 1992.

Granick, Eve Wheatcroft. *The Amish Quilt.* Good Books, Intercourse, PA, 1989.

Haas, J. Craig. *Readings from Mennonite Writings, New and Old.* Good Books, Intercourse, PA, 1992.

Haas, Craig and Steve Nolt. *The Mennonite Starter Kit: A Handy Guide for the New Mennonite.* Good Books, Intercourse, PA, 1993.

Hershberger, Guy F. *The Recovery of the Anabaptist Vision.* Herald Press, Scottdale, PA, 1957.

Hiebert, Clarence. *The Holdeman People.* William Carey Library, South Pasadena, CA, 1973.

Horst, Mary Ann. *My Old Order Mennonite Heritage.* PA Dutch Craft Shop, Kitchener, ON, 1972.

Hostetler, Beulah Stauffer. *American Mennonites and Protestant Movements.* Herald Press, Scottdale, PA, 1987.

Hostetler, John A. *Amish Life.* Herald Press, Scottdale, PA, 1983.

_____, ed. *Amish Roots.* Johns Hopkins University Press, Baltimore, MD, 1989.

_____. *Amish Society.* Johns Hopkins University Press, Baltimore, MD, 1993.

_____. *Hutterite Life.* Herald Press, Scottdale, PA, 1983.

_____. *Hutterite Society.* Johns Hopkins University Press, Baltimore, MD, 1974.

_____. *Mennonite Life.* Herald Press, Scottdale, PA, 1983.

Hostetler, John A. and Gertrude E. Huntington. *Amish Children.* Harcourt, Brace, Jovanovich College Publishers, 1992.

Hunsberger, David. et al. *People Apart.* Sand Hills Books, St. Jacobs, ON, 1977.

Hymnal, A Worship Book. Herald Press, Scottdale, PA, 1992.

Janzen, Jean. *Snake in the Parsonage.* Good Books, Intercourse, PA, 1995.

Janzen, Jean, Yorifumi Yaguchi, and David Waltner-Toews. *Three Mennonite Poets.* Good Books, Intercourse, PA, 1986.

Janzen, Reinhild Kauenhoven and John M. Janzen. *Mennonite Furniture: A Migrant Tradition.* Good Books. Intercourse, PA, 1991.

Jeschke, Marlin. *Discipling the Brother.* Herald Press, Scottdale, PA, 1972.

Juhnke, James C. *Vision, Doctrine, War: Mennonite Identity and Organization in America, 1890-1930.* Herald Press, Scottdale, PA, 1989.

Kasdorf, Julia. *Sleeping Preacher.* University of Pittsburgh Press, 1992.

Kauffman, J. Howard and Leo Driedger. *The Mennonite Mosaic.* Herald Press, Scottdale, PA, 1991.

Keim, Albert N. *The CPS Story: An Illustrated History of Civilian Public Service.* Good Books, Intercourse, PA, 1990.

_____. *Compulsory Education and the Amish.* Beacon Press, Boston, MA, 1975.

Klaassen, Walter. *Anabaptism: Neither Catholic nor Protestant.* Conrad Press, Waterloo, ON, 1972.

Kraybill, Donald B. *Passing on the Faith.* Good Books, Intercourse, PA, 1991.

_____. *The Puzzles of Amish Life.* Good Books, Intercourse, PA, 1990.

_____. *The Riddle of Amish Culture.* Johns Hopkins University Press, Baltimore, MD, 1989.

_____. *The Upside-Down Kingdom.* Herald Press, Scottdale, PA, 1990.

Kraybill, Donald B. and Phyllis Pellman Good. *The Perils of Professionalism.* Herald Press, Scottdale, PA, 1982.

Lesher, Emerson. *The Muppie Manual.* Good Books, Intercourse, PA, 1985.

Littell, Franklin H. *The Origins of Sectarian Protestantism.* Macmillan, New York, NY.

Longacre, Doris Janzen. *More-with-Less Cookbook.* Herald Press, Scottdale, PA, 1976.

MacMaster, Richard K. *Land, Piety, Peoplehood. The Establishment of Mennonite Communities in America, 1683-1790.* Herald Press, Scottdale, PA, 1985.

McCauley, Daniel and Kathryn McCauley. *Decorative Arts of the Amish of Lancaster County.* Good Books, Intercourse, PA, 1988.

Mennonite Confession of Faith. Herald Press, Scottdale, PA, 1963.

Mennonite Encyclopedia, The, Vol.1-5, Herald Press, Scottdale, PA, 1959, 1990.

Mennonite World Handbook. Mennonite World Conference, Kitchener, ON, 1990.

Miller, Levi. *Ben's Wayne.* Good Books, Intercourse, PA, 1989.

_____. *Our People: The Amish and Mennonites of Ohio.* Herald Press, Scottdale, PA, 1992.

Nisly, Paul W. *Sweeping Up the Heart.* Good Books, Intercourse, PA, 1992.

Nolt, Steven. *A History of the Amish.* Good Books, Intercourse, PA, 1992.

Ortíz, José and David Graybill. *Reflections of an Hispanic Mennonite.* Good Books, Intercourse, PA, 1989.

Oyer, John and Robert Kreider. *Mirror of the Martyrs.* Good Books, Intercourse, PA, 1990.

Pannabecker, S.F. *Open Doors: A History of the General Conference Mennonite Church.* Faith and Life Press, Newton, KS, 1975.

Peachey, Titus and Linda Gehman Peachey. *Seeking Peace.* Good Books, Intercourse, PA, 1991.

Pellman, Rachel and Kenneth Pellman. *A Treasury of Mennonite Quilts.* Good Books, Intercourse, PA, 1992.

_____. *The World of Amish Quilts.* Good Books, Intercourse, PA, 1984.

Redekop, Calvin. *The Free Church and Seductive Culture.* Herald Press, Scottdale, PA, 1970.

_____. *The Old Colony Mennonites.* Johns Hopkins University Press, Baltimore, MD, 1969.

Ruth, John. *Conrad Grebel, Son of Zurich.* Herald Press, Scottdale, PA, 1975.

_____. *Mennonite Identity and Literary Art.* Herald Press, Scottdale, PA, 1978.

Schlabach, Theron J. *Peace, Faith, Nation: Mennonites and Amish in Nineteenth-Century America.* Herald Press, Scottdale, PA, 1988.

Scott, Stephen. *The Amish Wedding & Other Special Occasions of the Old Order Communities*. Good Books, Intercourse, PA, 1988.

_____. *Plain Buggies*. Good Books, Intercourse, PA, 1981.

_____. *Why Do They Dress That Way?* Good Books, Intercourse, PA, 1986.

Shenk, Sara Wenger. *Why Not Celebrate!* Good Books, Intercourse, PA, 1987.

Showalter, Mary Emma. *Mennonite Community Cookbook*. Herald Press, Scottdale, PA, 1950.

Sider, Ronald J. *Rich Christians in an Age of Hunger*. Intervarsity Press, Downer's Grove, IL, 1977.

Smith, C. Henry. *The Story of the Mennonites*. Mennonite Publication Office, Newton, KS, 1981.

Smucker, Barbara. *Henry's Red Sea*. Herald Press, Scottdale, PA, 1965.

Society of Brothers. *Children in Community*. The Plough Publishing House, Rifton, NY, 1975.

Society of Brothers. *Sing Through the Day*. The Plough Publishing House, Rifton, NY, 1968.

Stambaugh, Sara. *I Hear the Reaper's Song*. Good Books, Intercourse, PA, 1984.

Stoesz, Edgar and Chester Raber. *Doing Good Better*. Good Books, Intercourse, PA, 1994.

Stoltzfus, Louise. *Amish Women*. Good Books, Intercourse, PA, 1994.

_____. *Two Amish Folk Artists: The Story of Henry Lapp and Barbara Ebersol*. Good Books, Intercourse, PA, 1995.

Toews, John A. *A History of the Mennonite Brethren Church*. Mennonite Brethren Publishers, Hillsboro, KS, 1975.

Voth, Norma Jost. *Mennonite Foods and Folkways, Vol. I-II,* Good Books, Intercourse, PA, 1990, 1991.

Weaver, J. Denny, *Becoming Anabaptist*. Herald Press, Scottdale, PA, 1987.

Wenger, J.C. *The Christian Faith*. Herald Press, Scottdale, PA, 1971.

_____. ed. Leonard Verduin, trans. *The Complete Writings of Menno Simons*. Herald Press, Scottdale, PA, 1956.

Wiebe, Rudy. *Blue Mountains of China*. McClelland and Stewart, Toronto, ON, 1975.

_____. *Peace Shall Destroy Many*. McClelland and Stewart, Toronto, ON, 1962.

Wittlinger, Carlton O. *Quest for Piety and Obedience*. Evangel Press, Nappanee, IN, 1978.

Yoder, John H. *The Politics of Jesus*. Eerdmans, Grand Rapids, MI, 1994.

_____. ed. and trans. *The Schleitheim Confession*. Herald Press, Scottdale, PA, 1977.

Yoder, Joseph W. *Rosanna of the Amish*. Herald Press, Scottdale, PA, 1995.

Index

About the Authors

Merle and Phyllis Good have teamed together on a host of projects through the years. For 25 years they have been co-directors of The People's Place, an educational and heritage center about Amish and Mennonite faith and life, in the village of Intercourse (Lancaster Co.), PA. They oversee several other projects in the village of Intercourse— The Old Country Store, The People's Place Quilt Museum, The People's Place Gallery, The Village Pottery, and Crafts of the World.

Both Goods are authors of numerous books; both have written extensively on Amish and Mennonite subjects. Their books have sold more than two million copies.

Among Phyllis' books are the beautiful photographic essay *Amish Children*, the children's book *Plain Pig's ABC's: A Day on Plain Pig's Amish Farm*, *The Best of Amish Cooking*, *The Best of Mennonite Fellowship Meals*, *A Mennonite Woman's Life*, and *Quilts from Two Valleys: Amish Quilts from the Big Valley, Mennonite Quilts from the Shenandoah Valley*.

Merle's books include the beautiful photographic essays *Who Are the Amish?* and *An Amish Portrait*, the novel *Hazel's People*, and children's books *Reuben and the Fire, Reuben and the Blizzard*, and *Reuben and the Quilt*. His Op-Ed essays have appeared in *The New York Times* and *The Washington Post*, among others.

The Goods work together each year to publish a thoughtful collection called *What Mennonites Are Thinking*.

The Goods live in Lancaster, Pennsylvania and are the parents of two young adult daughters. (All of their books are available from www.goodbks.com, or call 800/762-7171.)

Recommended

Readers should consider visiting an outstanding hands-on museum which explores the 20 most asked questions about the Amish and Mennonites. "20 Questions: A Discovery Museum for All Ages" is located at The People's Place, Intercourse, PA. Call 800/390-8436 for more details.
